'Sweaty palms? Racing heart? A lump in the back of your throat? As a maths teacher, I know that maths anxiety can prevent people, young and old, from accessing this beautiful subject. Judy draws upon her vast and rich experience in education to create this book that all teachers and parents should have. This engaging, fun and playful book has gathered together a wonderful collection of maths activities and curiosities that will engage maths fans but equally importantly, inspire those that need a little encouragement too!'

– Bobby Seagull, school maths teacher, author of The Life-Changing Magic of Numbers *and BBC presenter for the* Monkman & Seagull Genius Guides

'Judy has a genius for helping struggling learners enjoy numbers.'

– Professor Brian Butterworth, author of Dyscalculia: From Science to Education

'This is a cleverly organised, clearly presented collection of games and activities which will help build an understanding of maths in learners. It's a great example of "if you ask the right questions, the children learn".'

– Dr Steve Chinn, Visiting Professor, University of Derby

T0299620

Awesome Games and Activities for Kids with Numeracy Difficulties

How to Feel Smart and In Control about Doing Mathematics with a Neurodiverse Brain

Judy Hornigold

Illustrated by Joe Salerno

Jessica Kingsley Publishers
London and Philadelphia

First published in Great Britain in 2021 by Jessica Kingsley Publishers
An Hachette Company

1

Copyright © Judy Hornigold 2021
Illustrations copyright © Joe Salerno 2021

The fonts, layout and overall design of this book have been prepared according to dyslexia friendly principles. At JKP we aim to make our books' content accessible to as many readers as possible.

A CIP catalogue record for this title is available from the British Library and the Library of Congress

ISBN 978 1 78775 563 5
eISBN 978 1 78775 564 2

Printed and bound in Great Britain by TJ Books Ltd

Jessica Kingsley Publishers' policy is to use papers that are natural, renewable and recyclable products and made from wood grown in sustainable forests. The logging and manufacturing processes are expected to conform to the environmental regulations of the country of origin.

Jessica Kingsley Publishers
Carmelite House
50 Victoria Embankment
London EC4Y 0DZ

www.jkp.com

Contents

To Mrs Robin, the most inspiring maths teacher, who turned a very reluctant mathematician into one with a lifelong love and wonder of maths. I will be forever grateful for her enthusiasm and dedication.

Why I Wrote this Book

Have you ever felt anxious about maths? Or maybe you feel that you can't do maths and are worried about what people will think about you if you get the answer wrong.

Lots of people feel like this sometimes, and that is why I decided to write this book. When I was at school, I felt this way and I didn't enjoy maths at all. I didn't really understand it and it made me feel bad when I couldn't do it. But then something wonderful happened.

A new teacher arrived at the school called Mrs Robin, and she loved maths. She loved it so much that soon I grew to love it too.

I began playing with numbers and discovered the amazing patterns that they can make.

I stopped being frightened of making mistakes and started enjoying exploring numbers.

This love of maths has lasted my whole life and I am still finding out new things about numbers almost every day.

This book is a collection of some of the most awesome activities and curiosities in maths that I have enjoyed over the years. You don't need to be good at maths to do them, but you will need a calculator for some of them. You will also need a selection of family members and friends to amaze and astound with your incredible new maths knowledge.

I have split the book into nine chapters as I describe below, so amongst other things you can choose whether you want to be creative, play a game, impress your friends or simply be amused. The choice is yours.

I hope that you enjoy this book and that it will spark a love and fascination for maths.

How to Use this Book

This book is for you, to help you feel smarter when you do mathematics, and to empower you to realise all the fun you can have with numbers, so they don't feel scary any more. I have organised the games and activities into nine chapters.

You don't need to work through the chapters in order. You can pick and choose and just do what looks most intriguing or fun, or challenging (in a good way!) to you first. You can dip in and out of any chapter at any time.

Some of the games require the use of a calculator, but if you want a challenge, you can always play without a calculator. If you are going to use a calculator, see if you can have a good guess at what the answer may be before you plug in the numbers. Being able to roughly estimate in this way is a valuable skill when using a calculator as it will alert you to whether you have entered the numbers or operations incorrectly.

Chapter 1 (Play It!) and Chapter 2 (Play Some More!) are a collection of games using playing cards and dice, focusing mainly on the four operations. Games with playing cards are a great way of exploring numbers and finding out how numbers combine. They are also something you and your friends or your whole family can enjoy together.

Ponder It! (Chapter 3) introduces you to some of the mysterious numbers and patterns in the weird and wonderful world of maths. It is guaranteed to spark your curiosity and intrigue. Pattern spotting is a key skill in maths, and this chapter will encourage you to seek out patterns in numbers.

You can channel your inner magician in Chapter 4, Conjure It! The tricks in this chapter are a great way to build confidence in mathematics at the same time as impressing friends and family. If you feel that you are anxious about working with numbers, this is the chapter for you as it will make you feel that you are the most amazing mathematician on the planet!

Simplify It! – Chapter 5 – provides you with some shortcuts in numeracy; for example, how to tell what a number can be divided by and how to multiply by certain numbers. The tips in this chapter give you great ways to boost your confidence when multiplying and dividing.

Returning to the world of magic, but this time by looking at fascinating magic squares, Square It! – Chapter 6 – is one of my personal favourites! They may seem almost impossible to construct but in this chapter I show you how to make your own magic squares. Another way to impress friends and family!

Chapter 7, which I've called Make It! reminds us that maths is not all about number crunching. Many people find the spatial side of maths much easier to understand than the number side. The creativity in this area of mathematics is very satisfying to explore. You can explore tessellation and the work of Escher as well as making your own tessellating shape.

Chapter 8 (Riddle It!) is just for fun. It's a collection of jokes (some funnier than others) and a collection of riddles and mathematical picture puns. Maybe you can come up with some even better ones!

Believe It! – Chapter 9 – is where we look into some almost unbelievable maths facts – strange but true. You may be inspired to try to find out some more for yourself.

The templates that are required for some of the games can be found at the end of the book and can also be downloaded from www.jkp.com/catalogue/book/9781787755635.

An Introduction for Parents (and Interested Children)

Young children are naturally curious and endlessly playful. They have no fear of numbers and are intrigued by them. If you observe children in nursery or reception exploring numbers, you will find that they are often quite mischievous and experimental. They haven't learnt the rules associated with adding, subtracting, multiplying and dividing and are not bound by what they think the teacher wants them to do. They are not focused on getting the correct answer, nor doing the sum quickly and in their heads. They are simply having fun.

Sometimes they deliberately make a mistake to see how adults will react. For example, when asked to stand on the number 9 on a mat showing the numbers 1–100 one child stood on the number 23 and looked up with a cheeky grin. It wasn't that he thought 23 was the number 9, it was that he wanted to play a trick on the teacher to see what they would say. There was a 'glint in the eye joviality' in his play with numbers.

Young children often come up with sums like this:

$$1 + 0 + 0 + 0 + 0 + 0 + 0 + 0 + 0 + 0 + 0 + 0 +$$
$$0 + 0 + 0 + 0 + 0 + 0 + 0 + 0 + 0 + 0 + 0 + 0 +$$
$$0 + 0 + 0 + 0 + 0 + 0 + 0 + 0 + 0 + 0 + 0 + 0 +$$
$$0 + + 0 + 0 + 0 + 0 + 0 + 0 + 0 + 0 + 0 + 0 +$$
$$0 + 0 + 0 + 0 + 0 + 0 + 0 + 0 + 0 + 0 + + 0 +$$
$$0 + 0 + 0 + 0 + 0 + 0 + 0 + 0 + 0 + 0 + 0 + 0 +$$
$$0 + 0 + 0 + 0 + 0 + 0 + 0 + + 0 + 0 + 0 + 0 = 1$$

which they think is hilarious.

What an incredibly large sum they have done!

But actually, they have grasped an important concept about the effect of adding zero.

They enjoy making patterns like this:

$1 \times 1 = 1$
$1 \times 1 \times 2 = 2$
$1 \times 1 \times 1 \times 3 = 3$

1 x 1 x 1 x 1 x 4 = 4
1 x 1 x 1 x 1 x 1 x 5 = 5
etc.

These, and the different games and activities you will read about in this book, are fun things for children to do. But they also show that children can have a deep understanding of some important concepts in maths, such as the effect of multiplying a number by 1 or the effect of adding 0 to a number, even before we see them carrying out more obvious maths problems with confidence.

It is through exploration and play that young children can develop a deep, rich and long-lasting understanding of these concepts.

But as children go through school, they begin to learn that there are certain expectations and rules.

They learn that it is 'good' if you get the answer right and 'bad' if you get it wrong.

Children can then become anxious about making mistakes and there is a fear of appearing 'stupid' in front of their peers. So, for some children, unfortunately, the amusement and enjoyment of maths is replaced by anxiety and confusion. Maths becomes something to be avoided. But avoiding it is not an option. Just think about all the maths that we do, incidentally, every day.

Let's look at a typical day in a child's life and see just how much real maths a child is actually doing.

Adults, you can share this box with your child or other young children so they can see how maths is part of so much of what we do.

All the maths you do before you even leave the house!

— Woken up by your parents (or an alarm) at a set time every day. (This involves reading the time from a digital or analogue clock and also managing your time, for example, realising that you have to be dressed and ready to go in thirty minutes.)

— Breakfast – with timely reminders of how long you have until you leave for school. (This is building an appreciation of the passage of time.)

- If your parents are lucky, maybe you will help them lay the table for breakfast. How many plates or bowls do we need? (This shows you understand something called 1–1 correspondence.)

- How long will the toast take? (Time!)

- Is there enough milk for everyone to have cereal? (This involves both estimation and a sense of volume.)

- You now need to leave home in time to get to school. How long will the journey take? What time do you need to be at school? What time is it now? (Now you are reading digital and analogue time displays, and you are problem solving.)

And this is all before you have even got to school!

When a child is at school, there will be a daily maths lesson. Most children think that this is the only time that they are doing maths, but there are plenty of opportunities to add more maths into daily routines.

You could weigh their school bag. Which day of the week is their bag the heaviest?

Maybe you could time the walk to school. Or spot numbers on buses – will the next bus be a higher or lower number?

You could look for different types of numbers, odd numbers or square numbers in the houses that you pass on the way to school.

At school, they will have to line up. Who is first, second, third etc. Who is last?

In class, maybe they are sitting in groups of four. How many groups are there? How many children are in the class?

At home, how long do they spend on their homework? Is this longer or shorter than the time spent on their electronic devices? What is the difference between these two lengths of time?

Maths is all around us and we can bring it into our daily lives in ways that are not threatening, whether we are counting as we skip, sharing a pizza or playing games.

A note about dyscalculia

For some children, their difficulties with maths are due to a specific learning difference, dyscalculia. Dyscalculia affects around 5% of the population. It is a difficulty in understanding our number system and how numbers relate to each other. Children with dyscalculia find it very hard to compare numbers or to estimate amounts, and will have great difficulty recalling number facts and times tables.

Dyscalculia is present from birth and is a lifelong condition that is unrelated to IQ.

Children with dyscalculia will be anxious, even fearful, about maths and it can be really difficult to change this attitude. They will avoid it whenever possible, and this can make the problem worse as they are not getting the chance to develop their maths skills.

Stars scheme in this book

My reason for writing this book is to help all children to enjoy maths, whether they have dyscalculia or general maths difficulties, or even if they are just a bit fed up with maths.

The activities in this book will help a child to develop basic maths skills – without realising it! I have not aligned the activities to specific areas of the National Curriculum as this is not that sort of a book.

However, some of the games are starred, with one star being a relatively easy game progressing up to three stars for more complex games.

The aim of this book is to have fun with maths and to enjoy doing maths with friends and family.

There are no age limits on these games and they can be enjoyed across the generations.

This book will help you and your child to develop a sense of enjoyment in and curiosity about maths, and you will have plenty of fun along the way.

Chapter 1

Play It!

This chapter is full of games using playing cards.

Playing cards are a great resource to use when practising basic maths skills such as addition and multiplication, or even just for number recognition and ordering. They are also a good way to help you visualise what a number symbol actually represents as you can see the number symbols alongside an image of that number quantity.

Other advantages in using playing cards are that they are cheap, readily available and highly portable , so you can play these games when you are out and about or even when you are on holiday.

★ Order to ten

Why play this game?

This game will help with sequencing the numbers from 1–10. It is a good idea to vary this game so that you are ordering the numbers from greatest to smallest as well as smallest to greatest, as we often find it harder to learn to count backwards than forwards.

You will need

A pack of playing cards with the picture cards removed.

Picture cards are the Jack, Queen and King.

Sometimes the number 1 card is shown with an ace, but this is not a picture card so we can keep it in our pack.

This is a game for two to four players.

How to play

Shuffle the pack of cards and deal ten cards face down to each player. The dealer then shouts 'Go!' and each player must order their cards from smallest to greatest. If you have two cards with the same value, then you can place them in a stack.

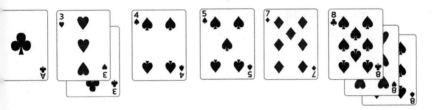

The first person to place their ten cards in the correct order is the winner.

Be creative
You can vary this game by having to order the cards from greatest to smallest, which can be a bit more challenging, or by sorting them into odd and even numbers.

★ Ten snap

Why play this game?
This game will help you to practise finding pairs of numbers that add to make 10. A lot of emphasis is placed on knowing the bonds to 10 and one of the reasons why this is important is because it is a really good strategy to use when we are adding numbers.

Try adding up these numbers in order from left to right.

$8 + 7 + 9 + 2 + 6 + 3 + 1 + 4$

Now try adding them up by looking for pairs of numbers that make 10.

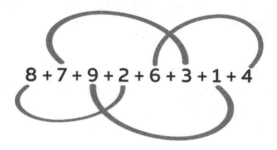

$$8 + 7 + 9 + 2 + 6 + 3 + 1 + 4$$

Much easier and much quicker!

You will need

A pack of playing cards with the picture cards removed.

This is a game for two players.

How to play

Shuffle the cards and deal out between the players. Then each player puts down a card in the centre so that they make two piles, one next to the other.

Instead of saying SNAP when you see two cards that are the same, this time you are looking for two cards that add up to 10. So you will say SNAP if the cards are 1 and 9, or 2 and 8 etc.

The winner is the person who ends up with all the cards.

Be creative

You can change the rules of this game to practise different skills. Maybe you can say SNAP when you see odd numbers, or numbers that add up to 12. Just use your imagination and be as creative as you like! This is a really good opportunity to develop number sense, through playing with numbers and exploring how numbers combine to make other numbers.

Did you know?

What are the chances of a shuffled pack of cards producing no SNAPs?

Well, it is 4.5%. This means that if you play SNAP 25 times, there will be one game where there is no SNAP!

★★ Spot the difference

Why play this game?

This game will help you to find the difference between two numbers. Finding the difference between two numbers can be tricky at first. There are various strategies that can be used, in particular counting on and counting back.

COUNTING ON

For example, to find the difference between 12 and 8 we may start at 8 and count on until we get to 12.

9, 10, 11, 12

Here we have counted on four times so the difference between 12 and 8 is 4. Be careful not to start the count at 8 as this will give you the answer 5!

8, 9, 10, 11, 12

COUNTING BACK

You can count back from 12 until you reach 8, but again be careful not to count the 12 as the first count.

11, 10, 9, 8

We have counted back four times so the difference between 12 and 8 is 4.

You will need
A pack of playing cards with the picture cards removed.

Dice.

How to play
Shuffle the cards and place them face up in four columns of 13 cards.

One player rolls the dice. Now, all players need to find pairs of cards that differ by the number shown on the dice. The pairs can be of any suit. Keep going until all the pairs with that difference have been found.

When no more pairs can be found, roll again and see if you can make more pairs.

Is it possible to remove every card?

K ♣	7 ♦	4 ♥	8 ♥
3 ♠	10 ♦	K ♥	2 ♣
1 ♠	8 ♣	3 ♥	6 ♦
Q ♣	10 ♥	4 ♣	Q ♥
5 ♥	2 ♠	8 ♦	7 ♥
J ♥	2 ♦	4 ♠	J ♣
3 ♣	5 ♦	8 ♠	K ♠
J ♦	10 ♠	3 ♣	1 ♥
2 ♥	9 ♦	Q ♦	9 ♣
J ♠	7 ♣	K ♦	5 ♠
6 ♠	4 ♦	1 ♣	1 ♦
10 ♣	7 ♠	3 ♦	Q ♠
9 ♥	6 ♣		

6 ♥	9 ♠

The winner is the player with the most pairs of cards.

💭 Be creative

Rather than subtracting, you could look for pairs of numbers that add to a given total. For this you will need to pick a number between 2 and 20, rather than rolling a dice. Try making up your own game, maybe use a 1–9 dice if you have one or make a 1–9 spinner. There are many variations that you can explore, and they will all help you to practise addition and subtraction skills and also to develop your mental arithmetic.

★★ Target practice

Why play this game?

This game will help you practise addition and subtraction. You can use a calculator if you want to, or you can write your running total on a piece of paper. If you want a challenge, try to do the calculations in your head and try to keep the running total in your head. It may take a bit of practice but it will help you develop your understanding of numbers and how numbers combine.

You will need
A pack of playing cards with the picture cards removed.

A calculator (optional).

How to play
This game is best played with no more than four players.

Shuffle the pack and deal out the cards between all the players.

Decide on a target number, for example 25.

Take it in turns to place a card face up on the table and keep a running total of the overturned cards. If the card played takes you over the target number, then you subtract that number. The winner is the first person to hit the target number exactly.

Be creative
You can vary this game by varying the target; a larger number will mean a longer game. If you are using a calculator, see if your child can estimate whether their card is going to take them over the target or not. They don't need to do the exact calculation, but it will help them to develop a feel for numbers if they can

predict whether they will exceed the total or not with each turn that they take.

★★ Salute!

Why play this game?

This game will help you learn your times tables. Learning your times tables can be hard work, and one of the best ways to help you to do this is to have plenty of practice. The more times we do something, the easier it becomes. Once you know your tables, it makes life easier when you are working on more difficult problems. Don't worry if you find this hard, lots of people do, but try to keep going and keep on practising.

You will need

A pack of cards with the picture cards removed.

This is a game for three players.

How to play

Two players sit opposite each other and the third player sits to the side.

Place the pack of cards face down on the table.

Players 1 and 2 both draw a card and place it on their foreheads, without looking at their card. They can see their opponent's card but not their own. The third player calls out what the product of the two cards is. From this call, each player has to work out what card they have. The first player to give a correct answer keeps both cards and play continues. For each round, the players take it in turns to be the caller.

Be creative

Can you change the rules of this game? You may want to start by selecting certain cards so that the children are only working with times tables that they are confident with. 1x, 2x, 5x and 10x are good starting points, and then move on to 3x, 4x and 6x. The 9x table has a lovely pattern so that may be worth trying next. The 7x and 8x usually cause the most trouble, so they can be practised when the child is confident with the other tables.

Maybe you could call out the sum of the two numbers instead. You could think about the difference between the two numbers, and this will give you more than one option so you could add clues to guide the players to the correct number.

Chapter 2

Play Some More!

This chapter has a selection of games that use dice, counters or digit cards. They will help you with your addition, subtraction, multiplication and division skills, without you even realising it! Why don't you stick post-its on the pages with the games you've enjoyed most, so you can remember to go back to them and try them with different groups of friends or family members?

Shut the box

Why play this game?
This is a great game for practising adding two or more numbers. There are commercially available versions of this popular game, but it is easy to make your own version.

You will need

Two dice and cards with the numbers 1 to 12 written on them.

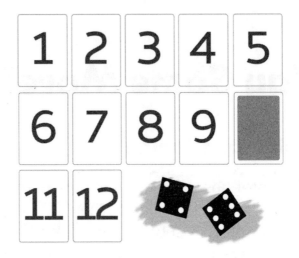

How to play

Start the game with all the numbers showing on the cards. The first player rolls the dice and turns over the card that shows the same number as the total shown on the dice. They can then roll again until they either throw a double or they can't turn over any cards. The cards that remain are added together and that is their score.

Now turn the cards again so that all of the numbers are showing, and the second player takes their turn. Decide how many rounds you want to play. The winner is the person with the lowest score after all the rounds have been completed.

Be creative
Try inventing new rules such as multiplying the remaining numbers or subtracting them from a certain number, say 50, to make the game more challenging.

Number bond splat

Why play this game?
This is a fun game for developing fluency in mental calculations.

You will need
Digit cards 0–9, blue tack, a 0–9 dice or spinner, and fly swatters.

This is a game for two players.

How to play
Blue-tack the digit cards on to a wall or large board.

Decide on a target number, no greater than 18, and then roll the 0–9 dice.

The aim is to find the number on the wall that will add to the number on the dice to make the target number. For example, if the target number is 9 and the dice shows 3 then 6 is the number to be swatted. The first player to swat the correct number is the winner.

💭 Be creative

You can vary this game by changing the target number or changing from addition to subtraction. You could use this to practise multiplication facts by choosing a target number that is in any times table up to 9 × 12. Then, roll the dice and swat the number that will multiply with the number on the dice to give the target number. If you feel that the speed element is adding to your child's anxiety then you can ignore that part and just give a star or award a point for each number correctly swatted.

★ Spotty dog

Why play this game?
This is a good game for practising addition and multiplication and for seeing the link between these two operations.

You will need
Blank dog templates (at the back of the book).

Counters for spots.

Dice.

How to play
First, roll the dice to see how many dog templates you will have. Roll the dice again to see how many spots to put on each dog. Then work out how many spots there are altogether.

Be creative
Try to come up with different ways of working out how many spots there are. For example, if you roll 3 and then 6, you will have 3 dogs each with 6 spots on them. The total number of dots could be found from adding 6 + 6 + 6, or it could be found from multiplying 3 × 6. This will help your child to make the link between addition and multiplication.

★ Spotty six

Why play this game?
This is a good game for practising number bonds.

You will need
3 x 3 grid (template at the back of the book).

Dice.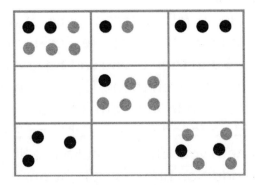

This is a game for two players.

How to play
The idea of the game is to make full boxes by drawing a total of six dots in each box. The first player to make a row of three full boxes, horizontally, vertically or diagonally, is the winner. Each player takes turns to roll the dice and to draw that number of dots in one of the boxes on the grid.

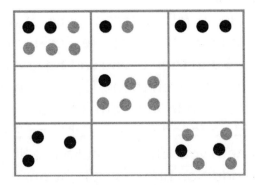

All of the dots from each throw of the dice must be put into one box. However, you can't have more than six dots in any one box. So, for example, if you throw a five, you can put five dots into an empty box or a box with one dot in it already, but you can't put them into a box with two or more dots in it already as this would make more than six dots in a box.

Be creative

This game can be easily modified by varying the number of dots allowed in a box. Can you find other ways to vary this game? Maybe you could change the dice that you use or change the number of sections in the grid.

Target 100

Why play this game?

This is a great game for practising multiplication facts, but also for thinking about strategy and developing estimation skills. You will need to think carefully about where you place your rectangles in order to maximise your chances of winning.

You will need

A blank 10 x 10 grid (template at the back of the book), two dice and two crayons of different colours.

How to play

The first player rolls two dice. Use these numbers to make an array.

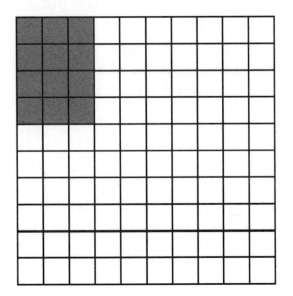

For example, if 3 and 4 are rolled then a 3 x 4 rectangle can be coloured in on the grid. Take it in turns to roll the dice and colour in arrays. The aim of the game is to colour in as much of the grid as possible.

The game ends when neither player can take a turn. The person who has coloured in the most squares wins.

Be creative

You can use different sized grids or different dice if you have them. You can change the criteria for winning so that the winner is the last person who is able to make a move.

★ Twenty

Why play this game?

This is a game of strategy – if you find a good strategy, you are sure to win! It will also help to develop mental addition fluency.

You will need

Counters.

This is a game for two players.

How to play

Each player has a pile of counters. Players take turns to place 1, 2 or 3 counters on the table. The player who places the 20th counter loses.

For example, a game may go like this:

Player 1 places 2 counters.

Player 2 places 3 counters.

Player 1 places 3 counters.

Player 2 places 3 counters.

Player 1 places 2 counters.

Player 2 places 3 counters.

Player 1 places 3 counters.

Player 2 loses as the next counter placed will be the 20th counter.

How to make sure that you win!

The key to this game is to make sure that you place the 19th counter. Then your opponent has to place the 20th counter. So how do you make sure that you reach 19 before your opponent?

In order to win the game, you need to get to these numbers on the way:

3, 7, 11, 15 and 19

So, a good strategy would be to start by placing 3 counters.

Then however many counters your opponent places, either 1, 2 or 3, you place the number of counters that will get you to 7, then 11, then 15 and finally 19.

Be creative

Try playing this game with a different target number. Do the winning steps differ if the target number is different? For example, what if you lose when the 24th counter is placed? Or the 25th?

★ Diffy game

Why play this game?

This is a game of strategy as well as a game for practising subtraction.

You will need

Diffy game board (template at the back of the book).

How to play

Start by writing four different numbers into the four circles on each of the outer corners of the grid. Fill in the outer squares by subtracting the smaller number from the larger number on each corner. Continue working towards the centre, subtracting the corners.

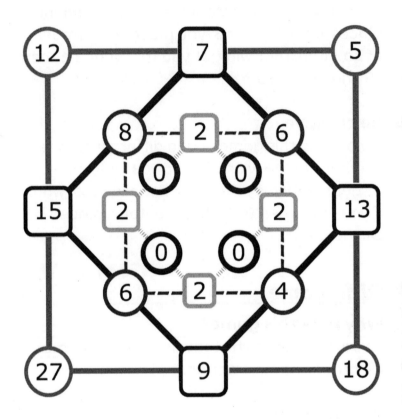

💭 Be creative

Vary the numbers that you start with. What effect does this have on the game?

What patterns do you see? Can you get to the middle without a difference of zero? How many steps does it take to get to zero?

Chapter 3

Ponder It!

This chapter explores some of the more mysterious numbers in maths.

You will need a calculator for this.

Sometimes I hear people complaining that maths is boring. Well, that's not true! It can be intriguing, confusing and very mysterious. Maths is full of patterns and connections. Some of them are predictable but others seem to come from nowhere. Here are a few of my favourite mysterious numbers and patterns in maths.

A word of explanation...or not!

For those who like explanations for everything! The explanations of some of these 'tricks' involve some very complex algebra that would not make any sense to most of us normal humans – where the trick is more easily explained, I give an explanation. Elsewhere, just enjoy the magic of the maths!

The number 37

Have you ever wondered what is so special about the number 37? Me neither! It looks like just another prime number (more on prime numbers later) and not a particularly interesting one at that. But look what happens when you multiply it by 3.

37 x 3 = 111

Is this really interesting?

Well, I think so because it means that if I multiply it by 6 (2 x 3) I will get 222 and if I multiply it by 9 (3 x 3) I will get 333.

Can you see the pattern? What do think will happen next?

37 x 3 = 111
37 x 6 = 222
37 x 9 = 333
37 x 12= 444

$$37 \times 15 = 555$$
$$37 \times 18 = 666$$
$$37 \times 21 = 777$$
$$37 \times 24 = 888$$
$$37 \times 27 = 999$$
$$37 \times 30 = ???$$

But that is not all that 37 can do!

You will need a calculator for this.

Step 1

Choose any number between 1 and 9 and press that button three times on the calculator.

Step 2

Press divide and enter the total of the numbers you can see on the screen.

Step 3

Press equals.

The answer will always be 37.

EXAMPLE
Let's try by entering 333.

$$3 + 3 + 3 = 9$$
$$333 \div 9 = 37$$

How about 555?

555 ÷ 15 = 37

Surely 111 won't work?

111 ÷ 3 = 37!

Prime numbers

So, it turns out that 37 is a pretty interesting prime number.

But what are prime numbers anyway?

A prime number has only two factors, 1 and the number itself. What does this look like?

Let's take eight counters and arrange them in rectangles.

 1x8

Or we could do this:

 2x4

8 isn't a prime number because we can make more than one rectangle.

Let's try this with 5.

 **1x5**

A rectangle of 1x5 is the only option – so 5 is a prime number.

Prime numbers are very important in maths. We can make any number we like by multiplying prime numbers together.

For example:

27 = 3 x 3 x 3
42 = 2 x 3 x 7

But they are also very mysterious as there is no pattern to them. They occur randomly in numbers, and mathematicians are still searching for undiscovered prime numbers.

On 7th December 2018, the Great Internet Mersenne Prime Search announced that a computer owned by Patrick Laroche in Ocala, Florida, had discovered a new prime number. At 24 862 048 digits, the number, known as

M82589933, is now the largest known prime number.

So how big is this number? At 24 862 048 digits long, it is nearly 1.5 million digits longer than the previous largest prime number. If you wrote it down, writing 1000 digits a day, it would take you 68 years to finish!

The search for new primes is highly competitive and there is a reward of $150 000 for anyone who can find a prime number with more than 100 000 000 digits. Good luck!

The 'primest' of prime numbers

Let's look at a somewhat smaller prime number: 733 939 133.

733 939 133 is an amazing prime. You could say it is the 'primest' number of all.

Let's take off the last digit.

> We now have 73 393 913
> 73 393 913 is still prime.
>
> Do it again to make 7 339 391
> 7 339 391 is still prime.
>
> Do it again to make 733 939
> 733 939 is still prime.

Keep on deleting the last number. Every number you make is still a prime number.

> **73 393**
> **7339**
> **733**
> **73**
> **7**

All prime numbers!

This is the largest known number that has this property.

Goldbach Conjecture

The **Goldbach Conjecture** is one of the oldest unsolved problems in maths. It states that every even integer greater than 2 is the sum of two prime numbers.

Here are a few examples:

    4 = 2 + 2
    6 = 3 + 3
    8 = 3 + 5
    10 = 3 + 7 or 5 + 5

It seems relatively simple but becomes much harder when we think about really large numbers. Can you think of two prime numbers that add up to 1 000 000? No? Me neither!

We know that the conjecture is true up to 400 000 000 000 000, but we are not sure yet that it is true for all even numbers. Some of the most powerful computers in the world are working on this problem.

Using prime numbers

Not only are prime numbers fascinating, they are also really useful.

Prime numbers are used to protect our bank accounts.

We have seen that we can multiply prime numbers together to produce other numbers, but splitting a large number into prime numbers is incredibly difficult to do, in fact almost impossible. So, these large numbers are used for codes to protect information. The large number is the 'lock' and the prime factors that multiply to make this number are the keys to the mathematical lock. This is how we protect our bank accounts and make sure that transactions online are secure.

Other fascinating numbers

Let's take 12 345 679 (all the digits 1–9 in order except for 8).

Enter this number into your calculator.

Now, multiply this by 8.

> 12345679 x 8 = 98765432
> Spooky!

Now try multiplying it by 9.

> 12345679 x 9 = 111111111

Try multiplying by other numbers – do you see any patterns?

Here's another curious pattern

> 0 x 9 + 1 = 1
> 1 x 9 + 2 = 11
> 12 x 9 + 3 = 111
> 123 x 9 + 4 = 1111
> 1234 x 9 + 5 = 11111
> 12345 x 9 + 6 = 111111
> 123456 x 9 + 7 = 1111111
> 1234567 x 9 + 8 = 11111111
> 12345678 x 9 + 9 = 111111111

What happens if we **start** with numbers that just have the digit 1 in them?

1 x 1 = 1
11 x 11 = 121
111 x 111 = 12321
1111 x 1111 = 1234321
11111 x 11111 = 123454321
111111 x 111111 = 12345654321
1111111 x 1111111 = 1234567654321
11111111 x 11111111 = 123456787654321
111111111 x 111111111 = 12345678987654321

All of these numbers are palindromes! So, multiplying a load of 1s by the same number of 1s will give us a palindrome.

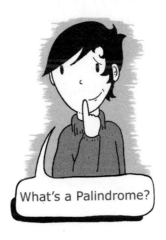

What's a Palindrome?

A palindrome is a word that reads the same forwards or backwards.

NOON, ROTOR, MUM are all palindromes.

Can you think of any more?

There are even some sentences that have this property.

A MAN A PLAN A CANAL PANAMA

Palindromes appear in numbers as well.

121, 12321, 543345

It's much easier to think of number palindromes than word palindromes.

In fact, if you take ANY number and add it to its reverse, you will get a palindrome. It may take a few steps but it always works!

Here are some examples.

Palindromes after one step:

$$
\begin{array}{r}
1234 \\
+4321 \\
\hline
5555
\end{array}
$$

Palindromes after two steps:

```
  3647            11110
 +7463           +01111
 11110           12221
```

Can you find any numbers that will take three steps to produce a palindrome?

Mysterious 1089

1089 is a very curious number indeed. Let's see what happens when we multiply it by the numbers 1–9.

1 x 1089 = **1089**	**9801** = 9 x 1089
2 x 1089 = **2178**	**8712** = 8 x 1089
3 x 1089 = **3267**	**7623** = 7 x 1089
4 x 1089 = **4536**	**6354** = 6 x 1089
5 x 1089 = **5445**	

Do you notice anything about the numbers in bold?

They are the reverse of each other – so as a pair they make a palindrome.

5 x 1089 makes its own palindrome of 5445.

What else is special about 1089?

Let's take a three-digit number, for example 276. Now reverse this number and find the difference between the two numbers.

$$672 - 276 = 396$$

Now add 396 to its reverse.

$$396 + 693 = 1089$$

This works for any three-digit number, as long as the first and third digits differ by at least 2.

Try it for yourself!

Other special numbers

We have seen that prime numbers are special, but there are other special numbers such as square numbers and triangular numbers.

Square numbers 1, 4, 9, 16, 25, 36, 49

Triangular numbers 1, 3, 6, 10, 15, 21, 28

When you multiply a number by itself the answer will be a square number. They are called square numbers because they make squares!

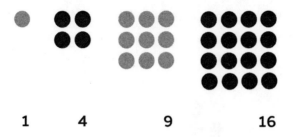

1   4   9   16

Triangular numbers make triangles.

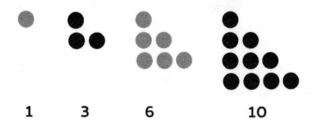

1   3   6   10

Let's see what happens if we add up odd numbers to make a sequence.

```
1                   = 1
1 + 3               = 4
1 + 3 + 5           = 9
1 + 3 + 5 + 7       = 16
1 + 3 + 5 + 7 + 9   = 25
```

What do you notice about 1, 4, 9, 16, 25?

That's correct, they are all square numbers.

How is that possible?

1 = 1x1

4 = 2x2

9 = 3x3

So, we can make squares from odd numbers.

We can also make squares from triangular numbers.

The triangular numbers are:

1   3   6   10   15

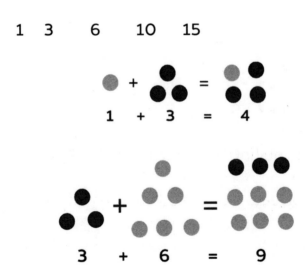

1 + 3 = 4

3 + 6 = 9

Another mysterious number is 142857

Strange, as this doesn't look very special. There is no real pattern there. However, this number was very intriguing for a certain Reverend Charles Dodgson, who was a Lecturer in Mathematics at Oxford University. He is better known as Lewis Carroll, author of *Alice's Adventures in Wonderland*. What Carroll noticed was that when you divide 1 by 7 you get a cyclical number (one where the sequence of digits repeats).

$$1 \div 7 = 0.142\ 857\ 142\ 857\ 142\ 857\ 142\ 857 \ldots$$

Furthermore, if you multiply 3 x 9 x 11 x 13 x 37 you will get 142 857.

37 popping up again!

Carroll discovered what happens when we multiply this number by 1, 2, 3, 4, 5 or 6.

142 857 x 1 = 142 857
142 857 x 2 = 285 714
142 857 x 3 = 428 571
142 857 x 4 = 571 428
142 857 x 5 = 714 285
142 857 x 6 = 857 142

Are you impressed? Well, what's so special? Can you see that all the answers have the same digits, but just in a different order? They may look different but in fact they are all in the same sequence.

142 857
428 571
285 714
857 142
571 428
714 285

Now let's add the digits up in groups of three.

$$142 + 857 = 999$$
$$428 + 571 = 999$$
$$285 + 714 = 999$$
$$857 + 142 = 999$$
$$571 + 428 = 999$$

and

$$714 + 285 = ??$$

Yes, you guessed it! 999.

Wow!!

So, what happens if we multiply 142 857 by 7?
Do you think the pattern will continue?

142 857 x 7 = ?

Try it and see.

Answer: 999 999.

Chapter 4

Conjure It!

This chapter is full of amazing tricks to dazzle your friends and family with. A lot of the tricks here use some of the mysterious numbers from Chapter 3, but there are a whole load of new magic numbers to explore as well. Most of these tricks take very little practice, but are very difficult for your audience to figure out. Some of the greatest magicians in the world base their tricks on the magic of numbers.

You will need a calculator for this.

We saw in the previous chapter how mysterious 1089 can be. Well, we can also use 1089 to perform some awesome magic tricks.

Mindreading book trick

You may have seen this trick performed on television and may have been astounded at the magician's powers. Now it is your turn to be that magician.

Step 1
Take any book and turn to page 10. Now count down 8 lines from the top and go along 9 words from left to right.

Write this word on a piece of paper and seal it in an envelope.

Step 2
Ask a friend to think of a three-digit number. The first and third digits need to differ by at least 2. Then ask them to reverse this number and find the difference between these two numbers. Now they need to reverse this number and add those two numbers.

Ask them to use the first two digits of their number and find that page in the book. Go down the number of rows indicated by the third digit and then across the line to the word located by the fourth digit of the number.

Open the envelope and you will have the same word!

How does this work?

Well, now that you are a fellow magician, I can share the magic with you – just make sure that you don't tell anyone else!

In the last chapter we started with a three-digit number whose first and third digits differed by at least 2.

Let's use 457. Now reverse this number and find the difference between the two numbers.

$$754 - 457 = 297$$

Now add 297 to its reverse.

$$297 + 792 = 1089$$

This will work for any three-digit number, as long as the first and third digits differ by at least 2. So when you play this trick, your friend or family member will always get the answer 1089, so they will always choose the ninth word on the eighth line of the tenth page.

Even and odd trick

You will need

Five cards with the even numbers 0, 2, 4, 6, 8 written in blue on the front and the odd numbers 1, 3, 5, 7, 9 written in red on the back.

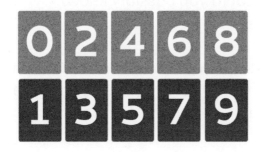

Step 1

Place the five cards on the table as shown in front of your friend or family member.

Step 2

Close your eyes or turn away and ask the other person to turn over some or all of the cards. It is entirely up to them. Now they just need to tell you how many **red** numbers they can see.

At this stage you can make a big deal about pretending to do some complicated maths in your head before you come up with a number. Tell them that the number you have calculated is the total of all the cards showing. Remember, you can't see the cards, so how could you possibly know?

Step 3
Well, all you need to do is add 20 to the number of red cards that they told you they could see.

So, for example, if your player says they can see 3 red cards, the total of all the cards will be 20 + 3 = 23.

If they say they can see 5 red cards, the total will be 25.

How does this work?
Well, let's assume that all the blue cards are face up. These cards total 20. For every red card showing we add 1 because each red card is one more than its corresponding blue card – simple!

Loop tricks

The next two tricks are all to do with numbers producing loops.

The 421 loop

YOU WILL NEED
A piece of paper with 4...2...1 written on it and sealed in an envelope.

Step 1
Ask a friend to pick a whole number and enter it into a calculator.

Step 2
If it is even, they divide by 2. If it is odd, they multiply by 3 and add 1.

Step 3
Repeat the process with the new number and do it again and again. What happens?

If they keep going, they will end up in a loop.

In fact, the sequence *always* ends in the 'loop': 4...2...1...4...2...1...

For example, let's start with 13.

13 is odd, so we multiply by 3 and add 1.

We get 40.

$$13 \times 3 = 39$$
$$39 + 1 = 40$$

40 is even, so we divide by 2.

$$40 \div 2 = 20$$

20 is even, so we divide by 2 and get 10.

10 is also even so we divide by 2 again and get 5.

5 is odd so we multiply by 3 and add 1. We get 16.

16 is even, so we divide by 2 and get 8.

8 is also even so we divide by 2 again and get 4.

4 is even so we divide by 2. We get 2.

2 is even, so we divide by 1 and get 1.

1 is odd, so we multiply by 3 and add 1. We get 4.

4 is even so we divide by 2. We get 2.

And so we begin the loop 4...2...1...4...2...1...

Step 4
Ask your friend to tell you the numbers in the loop that they have generated.

Now open the envelope for the big reveal!

Mystery loop!
Take any four-digit number, where the digits are not all the same (e.g. not 4444).

Let's use 1847.

Step 1
Arrange the digits in increasing order.

1478

Step 2
Arrange the digits in decreasing order.

8741

Step 3
Subtract the smaller number from the larger number.

8741 - 1478 = **7263**

Step 4
Now repeat this process with **7263**.

2367
7623
7623 - 2367 = 5256

REPEAT
2556
6552
6552 - 2556 = 3996

REPEAT
3699
9963
9963 - 3699 = 6264

REPEAT
2466
6642
6642 - 2466 = 4176

REPEAT
1467
7641
7641 - 1467 = 6174
7641 - 1467 = 6174
7641 - 1467 = 6174
7641 - 1467 = 6174 (we're in a loop!)

Amazingly, all four-digit numbers (not including multiples of 1111) end up in the 6174-loop. No one has yet found the reason why this happens!

Number generating tricks

The next three tricks will always produce the original number.

Number loop
Step 1
Ask your friend to think of a number between 1 and 100.

Step 2
Tell them to multiply this number by 3.

Step 3
Then add 6 to that number.

Step 4
Now they divide that number by 3.

Step 5
Finally, all they need to do is take 2 away from this number and they will have the original number.

EXAMPLE
I am thinking of 25.

Step 1
Multiply by 3.

$25 \times 3 = 75$

Step 2
Add 6.

$75 + 6 = 81$

Step 3
Divide by 3.

$81 \div 3 = 27$

Step 4
Subtract 2.

$27 - 2 = 25$

Try it out yourself!

Back to the start
This is a similar loop to the previous one, just with different steps.

Step 1
Ask your friend to pick any number.

Step 2
Tell them to add 30 to it.

Step 3
Then multiply this number by 2.

Step 4
Now subtract 4.

Step 5
Divide the answer by 2.

Step 6
Subtract 28.

They will always get back to your original number!

EXAMPLE
I choose 69.

Step 1
Add 30.

69 + 30 = 99

Step 2
Multiply by 2.

$99 \times 2 = 198$

Step 3
Subtract 4.

$198 - 4 = 194$

Step 4
Divide by 2.

$194 \div 2 = 97$

Step 5
Subtract 28.

$97 - 28 = 69!$

Favourite number generator
Step 1
Ask your friend to enter 12345679 into a calculator.

Step 2
Ask them to multiply this by their favourite number between 1 and 10. They can tell you what their favourite number is.

Step 3
Multiply the answer by 9.

Step 4
Now you can tell them what the calculator displays without even looking at it.

The trick here is that the calculator will display your friend's favourite number repeated nine times.

For example, if your friend's favourite number is 7 the calculation will be:

$$12345679 \times 7 \times 9 = 777\,777\,777$$

It works for any number.

$$12345679 \times 2 \times 9 = 222\,222\,222$$

So as long as you know their favourite number you will be able to astound them with your mental maths!

HOW DOES THIS WORK?
This works because 12 345 679 x 9 = 111 111 111. So all we are doing is multiplying 111 111 111 by their favourite single-digit number and we will get that number repeated.

Secret 73

Step 1
Write 73 on a piece of paper, fold the paper up and give it to a friend.

Step 2
Ask your friend to think of a four-digit number and enter this number twice into a calculator.

Step 3
Tell your friend that you know that their number will be divisible by 137 and ask them to check this on their calculator.

Step 4
Now ask them to divide this number by their original number.

Step 5
Ask them to look at your prediction on the piece of paper. It will match the number on the calculator.

How does this work?
Entering a four-digit number twice (12341234) is equivalent to multiplying it by 10 001.

$$1234 \times 10\ 001 = 12\ 341\ 234$$

Since 10 001 = 73 × 137, the eight-digit number will be divisible by 73, 137 and the original four-digit number.

Fab 4

Step 1
Ask a friend to write down a three-digit number.

Step 2
Now ask them to mix up the digits to get another three-digit number.

Step 3
Subtract the smaller number from the larger number.

Step 4
Add the digits in the answer. If the result of this is more than a single digit, add these digits together. Repeat until you end up with a single digit.

Step 5
Now subtract 5 from this number.

The answer is 4.

EXAMPLE

587

Mix this up.

785

Subtract the smaller number from the larger number.

```
  785
 -587
  198
```

Add the digits in the answer.

1 + 9 + 8 = 18

Keep adding until you get a single digit.

1 + 8 = 9

Subtract 5 from this number.

9 − 5 = 4

💭 **Be creative!**
You can use these steps to make any number by adding or taking different numbers away from 9.

Digit discovery

The next few tricks will all generate certain numbers.

Making 3
Step 1
Think of a number.

Step 2
Double your number.

Step 3
Add 6.

Step 4
Divide by 2.

Step 5
Take away the number you started with.

The answer will be always be 3.

LET'S CHECK THAT THIS WORKS
Step 1
I am thinking of 423.

Step 2
Double this number.

$$423 \times 2 = 846$$

Step 3
Add 6.

$$846 + 6 = 852$$

Step 4
Divide by 2.

$$852 \div 2 = 426$$

Step 5
Subtract the original number.

$$426 - 423 = 3$$

Making 5
Step 1
Write any three-digit number.

Step 2
Add that number to the next consecutive number.

Step 3
Add 9 to the total.

Step 4
Divide your answer by 2.

Step 5
Subtract your original number from the answer.

The answer will always be 5.

EXAMPLE
Step 1
I am thinking of 345.

Step 2
The next consecutive number is 346.

Add these numbers.

$$345 + 346 = 691$$

Step 3
Add 9.

$$691 + 9 = 700$$

Step 4
Divide by 2.

$$700 \div 2 = 350$$

Step 5
Subtract the original number.

$$350 - 345 = 5$$

You will always get 5!

Making 7
Step 1
Think of a number between 1 and 99.

Step 2
Double this number.

Step 3
Add 10.

Step 4
Subtract 3.

Step 5
Add 7.

Step 6
Divide by 2.

Step 7
Subtract your original number.

The answer will always be 7.

EXAMPLE

Step 1
I am thinking of 37.

Step 2
Double this.

$$37 \times 2 = 74$$

Step 3
Add 10.

$$74 + 10 = 84$$

Step 4
Subtract 3.

$$84 - 3 = 81$$

Step 5
Add 7.

$$81 + 7 = 88$$

Step 6
Divide by 2.

$$88 \div 2 = 44$$

Step 7
Subtract the original number.

$$44 - 37 = 7$$

It works every time!

Making 9
Step 1
Take a four-digit number.

Step 2
Write this number in reverse.

Step 3
Subtract the smaller number from the larger number.

Step 4
Add the digits of the answer.

Step 5
Then add the digits of that answer.

The answer will always be 9.

EXAMPLE
Step 1
I am thinking of 1234.

Step 2
Write this number in reverse.

4321

Step 3
Subtract the smaller number from the larger number.

$$\begin{array}{r} 4321 \\ -1234 \\ \hline 3087 \end{array}$$

Step 4
Add the digits of this answer.

$3 + 0 + 8 + 7 = 18$

Step 5
Add again.

$1 + 8 = 9$

Amazing number 9

Step 1
Ask your friend to write down a long number – it may be their telephone number or just a long number that they have made up. Make sure you can't see what they have written.

Step 2
Ask them to jumble up the digits in that number in any order they like and write down that number.

Step 3
Now they need to subtract the smaller of the two numbers from the larger one.

Step 4
Next, they need to add up the digits in the answer to this subtraction, and then add the digits in that answer.

Step 5
You now pretend to think very hard and tell them that the number they have is 9.

LET'S CHECK THAT THIS WORKS

Step 1
Original number.

74 562 398

Step 2
Jumbled up number.

23 896 457

Step 3
Subtract the smaller number from the larger one.

74 562 398 - 23 896 457 = 50 665 941

Step 4
Add the digits.

$5 + 0 + 6 + 6 + 5 + 9 + 4 + 1 = 36$

Step 5
Add these digits.

$3 + 6 = 9!$

It works every time.

Making 23

Now let's see if we can make two-digit numbers. What do we know about 23? Well, it is a prime number, but what else is special about 23?

Step 1
Choose any three-digit number.

Step 2
Add 25.

Step 3
Multiply the sum by 2.

Step 4
Subtract 4.

Step 5
Divide the answer by 2.

Step 6
Subtract your three-digit number.

You will always get 23.

LET'S CHECK THAT THIS WORKS
Step 1
I choose 123.

Step 2
Add 25.

$$123 + 25 = 148$$

Step 3
Multiply the sum by 2.

$$148 \times 2 = 296$$

Step 4
Subtract 4.

$$296 - 4 = 292$$

Step 5
Divide the answer by 2.

$$292 \div 2 = 146$$

Step 6
Subtract your three-digit number.

146 - 123 = 23

You will always get 23!

Animal magic

This is a great mind-reading trick to play on your friends. You will need the alphabet code sheet at the back of the book.

Step 1
Ask them to think of a number between 1 and 10.

Step 2
Now they multiply this number by 9. If the answer has two digits, they add those digits together.

Step 3
Now subtract 4 from their answer.

Step 4
Give them a code sheet.

A = 1
B = 2 etc.

Now, using this code ask them to think of an animal that begins with the letter their number matches in the code.

All you need to do now is to pretend to think very hard, as if you are reading their mind and say:

The animal you are thinking of is an elephant!

Three-digit repeating trick

Step 1
Ask your friend to enter any three-digit number into the calculator.

Step 2
Multiply it by 13.

Step 3
Multiply that answer by 7.

Step 4
Multiply that answer by 11.

What do they notice?

Does it always work?

Why does this work?
This trick works because we are multiplying our three-digit number by:

$$7 \times 11 \times 13$$

Now, $7 \times 11 \times 13 = 1001$.

So when you multiply a three-digit number by 1001, the three digits will repeat.

EXAMPLE

$$345 \times 1001 = 345\ 000 + 345 = 345\ 345$$

You can use this to impress your friends by giving them a calculator and asking them to plug in a three-digit number and show you that number. Then as quickly as they can they need to plug in x 7 x 11 x 13 into the calculator.

Whilst they do that you can write down the three-digit number twice.

You will have the same answer, but you will have been quicker than the calculator!

Try these out!
Enter a two-digit number and then press:

x 3 x 7 x 13 x 37

Enter a one-digit number and then press:

x 3 x 37

Enter a one-digit number and then press:

x 3 x 7 x 11 x 13 x 37

What do you notice?

Dice trick

Take two dice, the larger the better, and have some friends or family members in front of you.

Put the two dice together without looking and ask your friend what the numbers on the opposite ends of the joined-up dice are.

Now tell your audience that you know the total of the numbers that you can't see.

How does this work?
The total of the numbers hidden in the middle and the two end numbers will always be 14 because numbers on opposite faces of a dice add up to 7.

Dicey sevens

This is another way that you can impress your friends and family, whilst also practising the 7 times table!

You will need several dice and a plastic (opaque) cup.

Step 1
Ask your friend to place a number of dice (at least 2) in the cup. Tell them that you are going to race them to find the total of the numbers shown. All they have to do is roll the dice and add up the numbers shown on the dice. You, however, are going to add up the numbers showing on the dice and the numbers underneath that you can't see!

Step 2
As soon as they roll the dice you can shout out your answer since all you need to do is multiply the number of dice rolled by 7.

Calendar tricks

For this next section of tricks, all you will need is a calendar and a calculator. It doesn't matter which month or even which year your calendar is from.

Calendar capers

	1	2	3	4	5	6
7	8	9	10	11	12	13
14	15	16	17	18	19	20
21	22	23	24	25	26	27
28	29	30	31			

Ask your friend to draw a rectangle around any block of 20 numbers.

Now they need to add up these 20 numbers on a calculator.

While they do this, you add the smallest number in the block to the largest and then multiply by 10.

You will get to the answer way before your friend does.

It works every time!

LET'S CHECK THAT THIS WORKS
In our example the total will be 290 ((2 + 27) x 10).

Calculator conquest

Look away whilst your friend chooses one month from the calendar and draws a square that contains nine dates.

SUNDAY	MONDAY	TUESDAY	WEDNESDAY	THURSDAY	FRIDAY	SATURDAY
	1	2	3	4	5	6
7	8	9	10	11	12	13
14	15	16	17	18	19	20
21	22	23	24	25	26	27
28	29	30	31			

Now ask your friend to add up all these numbers on a calculator. Whilst they do this all you need to do is take the central number and multiply by 9. Write this number on a piece of paper and present it to your friend when they have finished their long calculation! They will be amazed!

Mental maths marvel
From a calendar choose a full week of seven days.

SUNDAY	MONDAY	TUESDAY	WEDNESDAY	THURSDAY	FRIDAY	SATURDAY
	1	2	3	4	5	6
7	8	9	10	11	12	13
14	15	16	17	18	19	20
21	22	23	24	25	26	27
28	29	30	31			

Tell your friend that you can add these numbers quicker in your head than they can with a calculator.

Ask them to tell you the date of the first day of the week that they have chosen.

All you need to do now is add 3 to that number and multiply by 7, then you will have the total of all the seven days.

EXAMPLE
First day of the week chosen is 12.

Add 3.

$12 + 3 = 15$

Multiply by 7.

$15 \times 7 = 105$

Check!

$12 + 13 + 14 + 15 + 16 + 17 + 18 = 105$

Birthday surprise

Step 1
Ask your friend to write down the month and day of their birthday.

For example, for 21st October they would write down:

1021

Step 2
Multiply the month by 5.

$10 \times 5 = 50$

Step 3
Add 6.

$$50 + 6 = 56$$

Step 4
Multiply this by 4.

$$56 \times 4 = 224$$

Step 5
Add 9.

$$224 + 9 = 233$$

Step 6
Multiply this by 5.

$$233 \times 5 = 1165$$

Step 7
Add the day of the month of your birthday.

$$1165 + 21 = 1186$$

Step 8
Your friend now tells you this final number.

Step 9
You subtract 165 from this number.

1186 − 165 = 1021
10/21

Their birthday is 21st October.

Finding the year you were born from your phone

It seems as though this would be impossible to do, but maths can be amazing at times!

Step 1
Ask your friend to write down the last four digits of their phone number.

Step 2
Now muddle up the digits to give a new number.

Step 3
Find the difference between these two numbers.

Step 4
Add up all the digits individually until you get a single digit.

Step 5
Add 16 to this result.

Step 6
Add this number to the year you were born.

Step 7
Tell me the final number.

Step 8
Now you take 25 away and that will give you the year of their birth.

Guess your age

This is a similar problem where you can find out someone's age without actually having to ask them!

Step 1
Ask your friend to add their age now to their age next year.

Step 2
Multiply this total by 5.

Step 3
Add the last digit of their year of birth.

Step 4
Subtract 5.

Step 5
Ask them to tell you this number.

Step 6
Now, you only need to take the first two digits of this number and it will be your friend's age.

Chapter 5

Simplify It!

This chapter is all about how to make life a little easier when we are doing maths. These are a few shortcuts that will help you when you are trying to work out if one number is divisible by another or if you need to find a quick way to do a multiplication.

Divisibility

How can you tell if a number is divisible by each of the numbers 2–12 if you don't have a calculator to hand?

This is another way to impress your friends and family with your amazing maths skills.

Divisor	Test
2	All even numbers divide by 2
3	Add up the digits in the number. If the answer is a multiple of 3 then the number is divisible by 3
4	Look at the last two digits of the number. If this number is divisible by 4 then the whole number is divisible by 4
5	Numbers that end in 0 or 5 are divisible by 5
6	Numbers that are even and have digits that add up to a multiple of 3 are divisible by 6
7	There is no specific test for divisibility by 7
8	Look at the number formed by the last three digits of the number. If this number is divisible by 8 then the whole number is also divisible by 8
9	Add up all the digits in the number. If the total is a multiple of 9 then the whole number is divisible by 9
10	Numbers with 0 as the final digit are divisible by 10
11	This is a more complicated test. Add up the first, third, fifth etc. digits. Now add up the second, fourth, sixth etc. digits. If the difference between these totals is 0 or a multiple of 11 then the number is divisible by 11
12	If the number is divisible both by 3 and by 4 using the rules given above then it is divisible by 12

Let's try this out on a large number, say 1 854 630.

The number ends in 0 so it is divisible by 2, 5 and 10.

The digits add up to:

$1 + 8 + 5 + 4 + 6 + 3 = 27$

A number is divisible by 3 if the sum of its digits is divisible by 3.

So, 1 854 630 is divisible by 2, 3, 5 and 10.

It is also divisible by 6 because it is an even number that is divisible by 3.

So, 1 854 630 is divisible by 2, 3, 5, 6 and 10.

Try it yourself!

Multiplication tricks

To multiply any two-digit number by 11, write the sum of the digits in-between those digits.

So for 34:

$3 + 4 = 7$, place the 7 between the 3 and 4
$34 × 11 = 374$

When the sum of the figures is more than 9, increase the left-hand number by 1.

So for 98:

9 + 8 = 17, add 1 to 9 to get 10; place the seven between the 10 and 8

98 × 11 = 1078

Mystery calculator

Show all six of the tables below to a friend and ask them to select any number from one of the six tables. Now they need to look for that number in the other tables. They will tell you which tables their number is in. All you need to do is add up the top-left corner numbers of those tables and you will have your friend's number.

Table 1

1	3	5	7	9	11	13	15
17	19	21	23	25	27	29	31
33	35	37	39	41	43	45	47
49	51	53	55	57	59	61	63

Table 2

2	3	6	7	10	11	14	15
18	19	22	23	26	27	30	31
34	35	38	39	42	43	46	47
50	51	54	55	58	59	62	63

Table 3

32	33	34	35	36	37	38	39
40	41	42	43	44	45	46	47
48	49	50	51	52	53	54	55
56	57	58	59	60	61	62	63

Table 4

4	5	6	7	12	13	14	15
20	21	22	23	28	29	30	31
36	37	38	39	44	45	46	47
52	53	54	55	60	61	62	63

Table 5

8	9	10	11	12	13	14	15
24	25	26	27	28	29	30	31
40	41	42	43	44	45	46	47
56	57	58	59	60	61	62	63

Table 6

16	17	18	19	20	21	22	23
24	25	26	27	28	29	30	31
48	49	50	51	52	53	54	55
56	57	58	59	60	61	62	63

EXAMPLE

If your friend chooses 27, this appears in Tables1, 2, 5 and 6.

So you need to add up 1 + 2 + 8 + 16 from the top-left corner of these tables.

1 + 2 + 8 + 16 = 27!

Try it out!

Chapter 6

Square It!

This chapter is all about magic squares. Magic squares are grids with a special arrangement of numbers. The numbers are arranged so that every row, column and diagonal adds up to the same number. 15 is the magic number in the square below.

8	1	6
3	5	7
4	9	2

There is another special number hiding in this square as well. Look at the numbers either side of the 5. What do they add up to?

It doesn't matter if you are looking to the left and right of the 5 or above and below it, or even at the diagonals. Each pair adds up to 10.

How long have we known about magic squares?

The earliest record of magic squares was in 2200 BC in China. Emperor Yu saw a magic square on the back of a divine tortoise in the Yellow River. In fact, the magic square that he saw is the same as the one above.

Let's have a look at some more magic squares.

16	3	2	13
5	10	11	8
9	6	7	12
4	15	14	1

16 + 3 + 2 + 13 = 34

16	3	2	13
5	10	11	8
9	6	7	12
4	15	14	1

16 + 5 + 9 + 4 = 34

As expected, the rows and columns add up to the same total. But this magic square has even more magic!

16	**3**	2	13
5	**10**	11	8
9	6	7	12
4	15	14	1

16 + 3 + 5 + 10 = 34

16	3	2	13
5	**10**	**11**	8
9	**6**	**7**	12
4	15	14	1

10 + 11 + 6 + 7 = 34

16	3	2	**13**
5	10	**11**	8
9	**6**	7	12
4	15	14	1

4 + 6 + 11 + 13 = 34

Sagrada Família magic square

There is a very famous magic square on the doors of the Sagrada Família Basilica (church) in Barcelona.

Can you see the magic?

The four numbers in the centre add up to 33. So do the rows, columns, diagonals and even the corners. Can you find any other groups of 4 that add up to 33?

33 is a very significant number for the church, as it is the age at which Jesus was crucified.

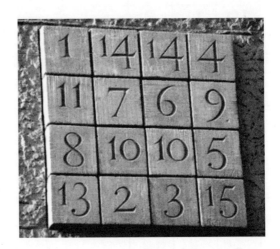

Upside down magic

This magic square works upside down as well! If you turn the square upside down or rotate the book through 180 degrees then the 'new' numbers still make a magic square, e.g. 81 becomes 18.

96	11	89	68
88	69	91	16
61	86	18	99
19	98	66	81

Upside down and back to front!

25	18	51	82
81	52	15	28
12	21	88	55
58	85	22	11

This square is even more special. Again, all the rows, columns and both diagonals add up to the same number (176) as do many groups of four (try adding up the four corners).

This time, turn the book upside down. The numbers on the square have changed, but it still works and they still add up to 176.

Now try looking at the reflection of the square in a mirror. Does this still work?

Wow!

Changeable magic square

8	11	2	1
1	2	7	12
3	4	9	6
10	5	4	3

This is a magic square that you can change so that the numbers in each row, column and diagonal add up to any number greater than 22.

For example, if you want the numbers to add to 32, you just add 10 to each of the grey numbers (because 32 is 10 more than 22).

If you want the numbers to add to 23, you just add 1 to each of the grey numbers (because 23 is 1 more than 22).

This is useful to know if you want to make a special birthday card for a relative.

8	11	20	1
19	2	7	12
3	22	9	6
10	5	4	21

Making a magic square

So, how easy is it to make a magic square? Well, actually, surprisingly easy!

Let's see if we can make a magic square that adds up to 19.

Step 1
Draw a 4 x 4 grid.

Step 2
Find any eight numbers that add up to 19. They don't all have to be different.

Step 3
Place the numbers along the top and down the left-hand side of the grid like this:

	1	2	0	3
4				
2				
3				
4				

Step 4

Now fill in the grid by adding the numbers at the top to the numbers at the side.

	1	2	0	3
4	5	6	4	7
2	3	4	2	5
3				
4				

Step 5

Now erase the numbers around the outside of the grid and your magic square is ready to use.

Step 6

Let's check the magic!

Choose exactly one number from each column and each row and you will find that they always add up to 19.

5	6	4	7
3	4	2	5
4	5	3	6
5	6	4	7

$5 + 4 + 4 + 6 = 19$

You can do this with any number; simply ensure the numbers across the top and down the side add up to your target number.

It's as easy as that!

Chapter 7

Make It!

Maths is found in many arts and crafts. This chapter is all about creating and making things using just a little bit of maths and some paper or card.

How to climb through a piece of paper

Now this is truly amazing!

You will need
An A4 piece of paper and a pair of scissors.

What to do
Ask you friends if they can cut a hole in the paper that will be big enough for them to climb through.

Impossible?

Well, you would think so.

Let them try for a while. You may need to use several pieces of paper!

When they get stuck or maybe even give up, all you need to do is take a piece of paper and follow these steps.

Step 1
Fold a piece of paper in half like a book. An A4 piece of paper is ideal.

Step 2
Cut into the folded side, about 1 cm from the right-hand edge, and start cutting straight towards the far side of the paper. Stop cutting about 1 cm before the opposite edge, so you don't cut all the way across the paper.

Step 3

Turn the paper around so the fold is away from you. Cut in around 1 cm from the last cut, and stop about 1 cm before you get to the folded side.

Step 4

Alternate between cutting from the folded side, and the side opposite. Keep your cuts 1 cm apart, and always stop cutting 1 cm before you get to the far side of the paper. When you have finished, you should have a zig-zag of paper.

Step 5

Now, be careful with this step. Look along the folded side of the paper. You should have a series of loops of paper. Cut along the fold of each of the loops, but make sure that you don't cut the first and last loops.

Step 6
Carefully, pull the loops apart to make a large loop that you can easily climb through.

Try it with a smaller piece of paper. How small can the paper be for you to still be able to climb through it?

Möbius strip

The Möbius strip is named after the mathematician August Möbius who invented the strip in 1858. It is curious because it only has one side. A Möbius strip is simple to construct.

You will need
All you need is a long strip of paper, sticky tape and a pair of scissors.

Step 1

Take the long piece of paper and put the ends together as if you were making a headband. Before you attach the two ends with tape, give one of them a twist and then stick the ends together.

Step 2

Now try drawing a line along the centre of the strip. What do you notice?

You will end up back where you started, without having to take your pen off the paper. So you have drawn on both sides of the strip of paper in one go, meaning that your original strip of paper, which had two sides, now only has one side!

Step 3

Now cut along the line that you have drawn. What do you think might happen?

Try it and see!

There are many other interesting things that you can do with this strip. Try making another one, but this time instead of cutting along the middle, cut a third of the way from one edge. What do you think will happen this time?

What happens if you make two twists in the paper?

Have fun exploring this and see if you can predict what will happen.

Magic paper clip trick

You will need
Paper, a pair of scissors and two paper clips.

Step 1
Cut a strip of paper that is about 5 cm wide and 30 cm long.

Step 2
Curve it round into an S shape and place two paper clips as shown below.

Step 3
Now impress your friends and family by telling them that you are going to join the two paper clips together without touching them. You will only be using the power of your mind.

Step 4
Pull the ends of the paper outwards with a sharp snap. The paper clips will join together and fly off the paper.

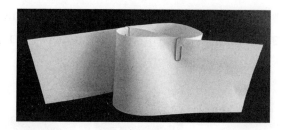

Tangrams

Tangrams were invented in China approximately 200 years ago. They are made by cutting a square into seven pieces.

Each tangram puzzle contains the following:

- two large right-angle triangles
- one medium-sized right-angle triangle
- two small right-angle triangles
- one small square
- one parallelogram.

How to play

Copy the Tangram template on p.144 onto card and cut carefully along the lines. You can colour the pieces if you want to.

Can you use the seven pieces to make the pictures shown below?

Can you come up with your own designs?

Challenge your family and friends to make different shapes or animals. You can find lots online including on Pinterest.

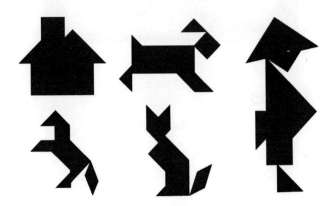

Tessellations

A tessellation is a pattern of 2D shapes which fit perfectly together, without any gaps.

Escher tessellations

M.C. Escher was born in 1898 in the Netherlands. He was known for his incredible tessellating art.

Do an internet search for some examples of his work. It's amazing.

How to tesselate any shape

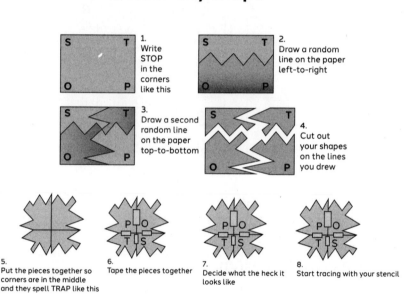

Adapted from Mathengaged.org

Once you have made your tessellating shape you could try to style it into a creature, a monster or even an alien! What does your shape look like to you?

Perfect patchwork

You can make a paper pattern or, if you are good with a needle and thread, you could even make a quilt or a cushion cover.

You will need

Paper or fabric squares.

These are six ways that you can cut the squares to make patchwork pieces.

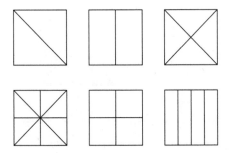

Decide on how you want to cut your squares and then have fun piecing them together.

Here are a few examples.

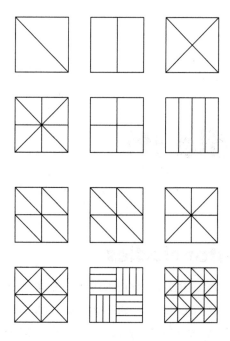

Can you find any other ways to make different patterns?

Chapter 8

Riddle It!

Calculator riddles

Use your calculator to solve these riddles. Enter the calculation shown into your calculator then turn your calculator upside down to reveal the answer.

1. When a crab is surprised it has _____ shock.

   93 528 -16 183

2. At the end of a lesson the school _____ rings.

   3122 + 4616

3. A spider has eight _____ .

   3295 + 2342

4. The opposite of more: _____.

9463 - 3926

Try making up your own riddles using this code

0 = O
1 = I
2 = Z
3 = E
4 = H
5 = S
6 = G
7 = L
8 = B
9 = G

You will need to write your word backwards so that it is the right way around when you turn the calculator upside down.

Maths jokes

Here is a selection of my favourite maths jokes. Can you come up with any of your own? Or find some online to try out on your friends?

Why do plants hate maths?
Because it gives them square roots!

What did the zero say to the eight?
'Nice belt!'

Why should you worry about the maths teacher holding graph paper?
She's definitely plotting something.

What do you call a number that just can't keep still?
A roamin' numeral.

Why is it sad that parallel lines have so much in common?
Because they'll never meet.

Are monsters good at maths?
Not unless you Count Dracula.

Why are obtuse angles so sad?
Because they're never right.

Did you hear about the mathematician who was afraid of negative numbers?
He would stop at nothing to avoid them.

How do you stay warm in any room?
Just huddle in the corner, where it's always 90 degrees.

A farmer counted 297 cows in the field.
But when he rounded them up, he had 300.

Why did the chicken cross the Möbius strip?
To get to the same side.

What's the best place to do maths homework?
On a multiplication table.

Why is six afraid of seven?
Because seven eight nine.

Why did the obtuse angle go to the beach?
Because it was over 90 degrees.

Why should you never argue with decimals?
Decimals always have a point.

Who invented the Round Table?
Sir Cumference.

Maths limerick

There was once a young lady called Bright
Who travelled much faster than light
She woke up one day
In the usual way
And returned the previous night.

Chapter 9

Believe It!

Shuffling cards

Have you ever wondered how many ways there are to shuffle a pack of cards?

More than a million?

More than a billion?

Surely not that many!!!

Well, in fact there are

80 000 000 000 000 000 000 000 000 000
000 000 000 000 000 000 000 000
000 000 000 000 000 000 (67 zeros!!!)

ways to arrange a deck of 52 cards.

That's a huge number, roughly equal to the number of atoms in our galaxy.

This means that any time you shuffle a pack of cards, it is almost certain that no one has ever shuffled a pack in exactly that way before and may never do it exactly that way again.

How clever of you to come up with such a unique way to shuffle the pack!

James Bond Casino Royale

For any James Bond fans out there, you may remember a scene in *Casino Royale* when James Bond is playing poker with Le Chiffre. Both men think they have a winning hand. How likely is it that they could both have such winning hands?

We need to look at the probability of each hand for the four players.

Player 1 has a Flush
Player 2 has a Full House
Player 3 has a Full House
Player 4 has a Straight Flush

The probability for each hand is:

Straight Flush: 0.0311%
Full House: 2.60%
Flush: 3.03%

So:

0.000311 x 0.026 x 0.026 x 0.03 =
0.00000000630708

And 1.0 / 0.00000000630708 = 158 551 976

So this could happen 1 in 158 551 976 times.

In other words, these players would have to play nearly 160 million games for this scenario to happen.

In fact, it is surprisingly easy to generate enormously large numbers from very small beginnings.

All the rice in the world

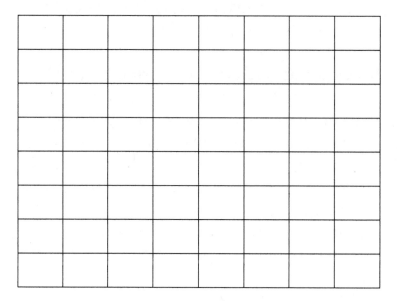

This is an old legend about a very wise servant and how he tricked his master.

The servant had been very loyal and brave so the master wanted to reward him. The servant thought hard before asking for just one thing.

All he wanted was for the master to give him one grain of rice put on a square of a chessboard on one day and then two grains on the next square on the next day, four grains on the next square on the next day, with the grains of rice doubling each day until all the squares of the chess board had been used up.

The master was surprised at the servant's request. It seemed like a very small price to pay for such loyalty and bravery.

So was this such a small price to pay?

On day 1 the servant has one grain of rice and this doubles each day. By day 8 the servant has 128 grains of rice, which does not seem very much. However, by the time day 64 comes along the servant would have 18 446 744 073 709 551 615 grains of rice. This is an almost unimaginable number. So let's see how much this amount of rice would weigh.

1 tonne of rice contains around 10 000 000 grains of rice.

Our servant would have
72 057 594 037 927 936 tonnes of rice.

How can we read such a large number? Well, let's find out the names for these really large numbers.

Million = 1 000 000
Billion = 1 000 000 000
Trillion = 1 000 000 000 000
Quadrillion = 1 000 000 000 000 000

So here we have 72 quadrillion tonnes of rice. This is more rice than there is in the whole world – so the servant was very wise indeed!

Templates for games

These templates can be downloaded from www.jkp.com/catalogue/book/9781787755635

10 x 10 grid

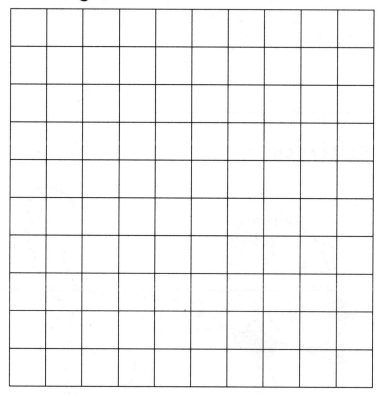

3 × 3 grid

Spotty dog

Diffy game

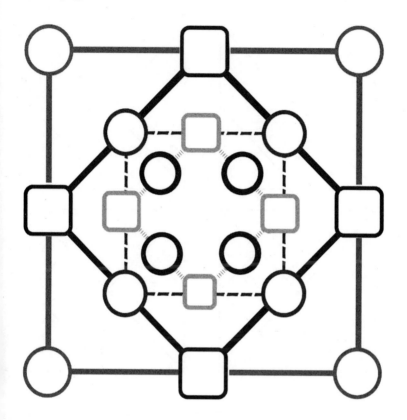

Alphabet code sheet

A = 1	J = 10	S = 19
B = 2	K = 11	T = 20
C = 3	L = 12	U = 21
D = 4	M = 13	V = 22
E = 5	N = 14	W = 23
F = 6	O = 15	X = 24
G = 7	P = 16	Y = 25
H = 8	Q = 17	Z = 26
I = 9	R = 18	

Tangram template

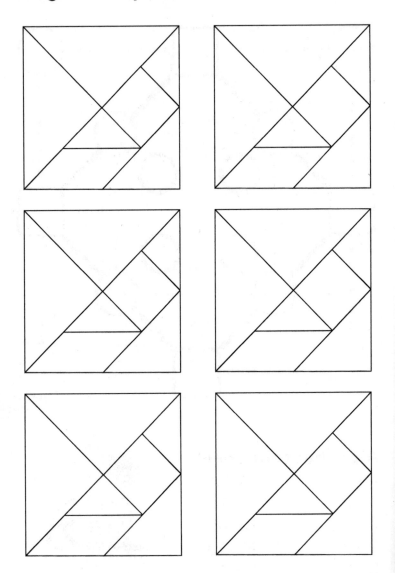